Financial Management:

Ratio Analyses

Copyright ©2017 by Chrys Brobbey
chrysbywriter@netzero.net

All rights reserved.

No part of this book may be used or reproduced in any manner without prior permission from the copyright owner except for use in reviews, research or academia.

High Hills Publishing LLC

FINANCIAL MANAGEMENT:

Ratio Analyses

by
Chrys Brobbey

This Book is for the use of:

Those in Pursuit of Knowledge and Excellence

in Matters of Management and Finance.

Quotes on Finance

"Being rich is a good thing. Not just in the obvious sense of benefitting you and your family, but in the broader sense. Profits are not a zero sum game. The more you make, the more of a financial impact you can have."

Mark Cuban

"I finally know what distinguishes man from the other beasts: financial worries."

Jules Renard

"Governments must commit to sound economic and financial policies. This is how we ensure reform in the euro area - and our independence."

Mario Draghi

"A penny saved is a penny earned."

Benjamin Franklin

"We teach about how to drive to school, but not how to manage finances."

Andy Williams

"When you work on something that only has the capacity to make you 5 Dollars, it does not matter how much harder you work – the most you will make is 5 Dollars."

Idowu Koyenika

"Money, like emotions, is something you must control to keep your life on the right track." *Natasha Munson*

Foreword.

This book is not meant as a textbook, because I am not basing it on any curriculum or syllabus. Instead, it is the synthesis of my study and work experience. In that context, a little information about me at this point will be in order. I have an extensive and varied working career. I hold a Bachelor's in Administration (Accounting option), and a Masters in Organizational Management. On completion of my first degree course, I worked at the then Coopers & Lybrands (now merged with PriceWaterhouseCoopers). Whilst there I was involved in the audit of the accounts of insurance, manufacturing, automobile, oil, banks, and other companies. Afterwards, I worked for over ten years with Nestle Foods as cost accountant in one of their manufacturing units, and later with a retirement community as director of accounting. The knowledge that I acquired in these various positions is what I present in this book. It is, therefore, suited for the consumption and application of people working in those fields, as well as for students of Finance and Accounting. I have also included in *'Section Two'* under 'Organizational Management' topics from some academic papers that I worked on. I've also listed at the end the novel and poetry books that I have published, and a synopsis of each. I hope readers will derive much satisfaction in browsing through this volume.

Section 1

Financial Analyses:

Profitability Ratios

Liquidity Ratios

Coverage Ratios

Leverage Ratios

Section 2

Organizational Management:

Organizations as Organisms within Cultures

Re-engineering the Dysfunctional Organization

An Analysis of the Book "The Tao of Leadership"
by John Heider

Section 3

Leadership in a Dictatorship:
A Classic Case of Ruthlessness

SECTION 1

Diagnosing the Health of an Organization by means of

FINANCIAL ANALYSES

Financial Analyses

Success in any business or undertaking is measured against the achievement of pre-established goals. In any enterprise management has the responsibility of setting up the yardstick against which performance can be evaluated. The goals of management are stated in a business budget, similar to the manifesto of a political party running in elections for the governance of a country or state. At periodic intervals actual performance is weighed against the set goals to gauge the measure of success. This serves as a mirror, like someone dressing up for an important event, to fine-tune any possible glitches in look. Management is thus able to make needed tweaks and adjustments to performance to be on course to the realization of the targets set.

Planning:

The above process is generally known as 'Planning.' It has been funnily stated by Alan Lakein that "Failing to plan is planning to fail." So the management of any public or private organization has no option but to plan, or suffer collapse.

For the financial manager planning is the key to success. Good financial plans must take into account the organization's existing strengths and weaknesses. It is like a physician taking into consideration a patient's genetic projection in order to prescribe a holistic regime of treatment. And just as the physician determines the health of the patient by means of laboratory tests, the financial manager uses the tools of financial analyses to determine if budget standards are being met. Financial analysis may also be carried out by other interested parties – creditors, investors, tax authority, and auditors – to safeguard their interest.

Financial Ratios:

The yardstick usually used to judge the performance of a company is a *ratio*, or an *index*. A ratio relates two pieces of data to each other. As an example, the ratio of women to men working in a grocery store may be found to be *2:1;* showing that for every male hired there are two females hired as well. This may be the norm in some professions, such as in nursing and teaching. An analysis and interpretation of various ratios give a better understanding of the financial condition of a company. Analyses allow for two types of comparison:

Firstly, present ratios can be compared with past ratios of the same company. For example, the ratio for the current year-end could be compared with the same ratio for the preceding year-end and past years to determine a trend. In this way the direction of change will show whether there has been an improvement or a worsening in the financial state and performance of the company. It serves as a monitoring tool for management; either a wake-up call, or a congratulatory pat.

Secondly, the company's ratios can be compared with those of similar firms or with industry standards at the same point in time. For any such inter-company or industry comparison to be meaningful the methods of accounting used by the different companies must be similar. To ensure such conformity, generally accepted accounting principles, referred to by acronym as GAAP have been established. They are the standards that every reputable company is expected to follow. This allows for the matching of apples with apples and oranges with oranges, and not apples with oranges. Such comparisons offer insight into the financial health and performance of a company relative to similar companies. This is similar to the medical report where the patient's numbers are compared with the standard range numbers to isolate deviations that call for attention.

Types of Ratios

There are as many financial ratios as the analyst's ingenuity can make up. The ratio is essentially a tool to serve a need, so the analyst may try to devise his own or used customized ones already available. In general the existing ones cover most conceivable needs, so analysts tend to rely on them rather than waste time and resources to invent the wheel. Each particular analysis has a purpose or use, and that determines the focus on what ratios to compute. The approach depends on who is interested in the analyses: third parties or management. Management is, of course, interested in all the financial ratios of the company. Aside from the analyses serving as tools for internal control, management must be concerned with the factors that outsiders rely on to evaluate the risk of doing business with the company. The financial analyses are part of the broader information processing machinery on which informed and sound decisions can be based. For that matter a solid management accounting (with cost accounting) unit in an organization is the surest bet to crunching the data from the financial accounting unit to ensure that prompt corrective measures are in place to check deviations.

The major standard types of ratio analyses fall under the following:
- ***Profitability Ratios***
- ***Liquidity Ratios***
- ***Coverage (or Activity) Ratios***
- ***Leverage (or Debt) Ratios***

The composition of each of these, their importance and uses require an analysis as detailed on the pages that follow.

PROFITABILITY RATIOS:

Profitability is the crux of any organization, without which the company would cease to exist. Even an acknowledged Not-for-Profit company must still be profitable, or at the least operate at break-even level to continue in existence. Hence management's greatest burden is to ensure profitability, or survival. The decisions of management and their efficiency in operations determine profitability. There are two classes of profitability ratios:

1) **Profitability in relation to Sales**
2) **Profitability in relation to Investment (Assets)**

The results of the two indicate the efficiency of management decisions and the operations of the company. There are any numbers of these ratios that can be formulated. The common ones are discussed below.

1) Profitability in relation to Sales:

(a) Gross Profit Margin

The Gross Profit Margin shows profit in relation to sales, after deducting the Cost of Goods Sold (COGS), but before accounting for selling and administrative expenses. It shows the efficiency of pricing decisions as well as production operations. The formula is as follows:

$$\frac{\text{Gross Profit}}{\text{Sales}} \quad \text{OR} \quad \frac{\text{Sales - COGS}}{\text{Sales}}$$

Eg: G.P: $\frac{\$1755}{\text{Sales: } \$3000}$ G.P: $\frac{\$(3000 - 1245)}{\text{Sales: } \$3000}$

Gross Profit Margin = ***0.585***
i.e **58.5%**

The ratio above means that 58.5% of sales revenue will go to cater for the other expenses not directly related to production, with any leftover being the net profit. This margin can be compared to that of the prior year to see a trend – either downwards or upwards. Or it can be compared to that of similar companies in the industry, or the industrial average. But, more important, it will be compared to what has been forecast for the period; and if there is a shortfall the management will have to investigate and initiate measures for improvement on future outcomes. In my experience as cost accountant, this was done by analyzing variances in direct production inputs, such as raw materials, labor, energy and production overheads.

(b) Net Profit Margin

The Net Profit Margin shows the efficiency of the operations of a company after taking into account all the expenses incurred in earning the revenue in question. The margin shows the profit arising out of every $1.00 of sales. The calculation is as per the example below:

<u>Net Profit</u>
　Sales

Eg:　Sales　　　$3000　　N.P:　　$ 750
　　　Net Profit: $ 750　　Sales:　$3000

$$\text{Net Profit Margin} = \mathbf{0.25}$$
$$\text{i.e } \mathbf{25.0\%}$$

This hypothetical case illustrates that for every $1.00 of sales, the result achieved is $0.25 in profit; that is $0.75 covers the expenses of production, selling and administrative expenses and tax for the period. This result will be compared with what is budgeted as the expected net profit, and analyses made of material variances to find out the causes. Moreover, this margin can be compared with the industrial average. In this case, assuming that the industrial norm is **30.0%**, then this company's margin is clearly below the expected, and management will have to find out why, especially if it is below that budgeted by the company as well. And, really, hardly will any company set its budget below the industrial standard. Else, the company cannot be competitive in the industry, and may be the first to fold up when the industry in general experiences hard times. Where in any year a company's realized margin falls below its budgeted, the reason could be due to any one of the following reasons, or a combination of both:
1) Comparatively low prices
2) Comparatively high costs

Effect of Gross Profit & Net Profit Margins

The importance of both the Net and Gross Profit Margins is that they indicate the strengths of the company, and to what extent it can withstand economic bad times. In the case above, the statistics are as follows:

		$	%
a)	Sales Income:	3,000	100.0
b)	Cost of Goods Sold:	1,245	41.5
c)	Gross Profit:	1,755	58.5
d)	Selling/Admin. Exps.:	805	26.8
e)	Net Profit before Tax:	1,000	33.3
f)	Tax @ 25% of N.P:	250	8.3
g)	Net Profit after Tax:	750	25.0

By the figures above, if direct costs of goods sold increase by $1000, approximately 80% (1000/1245), the company will just break even, with selling/admin expenses remaining the same. And, where cost of goods sold remain same, an increase in selling/admin expenses by over 124% (1000/805) will still see the company at breakeven. Management will, thus, have to examine the impact of any decision making with respect to increases in costs, not matched by equal or higher increase in sales, on the overall results. Also, where selling price decreases are not matched by decreases in costs, the company's profit margin will be negatively impacted. These profit margins thus serve as useful benchmarks in assessing the degree of safeguard against losses arising from rising costs and/or falling prices.

The interplay of the Net and Gross Profit margins over periods may be used as diagnostic tools into the operations of the company:
1) Where the Gross Profit Margin remains the same or close over a period of time, but the Net Profit Margin falls over the same period of time, then the obvious reason is increases in selling/ admin expenses. These expenses have to be analyzed and corrective actions taken.
2) Where the Gross Profit Margin falls, but the Net Profit Margin remains unchanged over the same period of time, the clear causes are increase in costs of production and/or cost factors if selling prices remain the same.

Changes in the Net and Gross Profit margins overtime could be due to any number of factors. To pinpoint the specific factors, we need to examine the specific costs components, such as labor, energy, materials and the various overhead items. This will reveal the areas with much impact on the changes, and that call for scrutiny and action. In such a case, the managers responsible for those cost centers will be tasked to explain the variations. To avoid censure, responsible managers monitor their cost inputs continuously over the operational cycle to correct and keep spending or usages within budget. It is for this reason that some managers are tempted to overstate their budgets in order to have operational leeway. In my position as cost accountant coordinating the overall budget preparation, I had this at the back of my mind and got the departmental managers to justify every line item, where comparison with prior estimates and actuals showed much disparity after allowing for reasonable margin of losses. To be effective in this role and act without fear or favor, the budget coordinator must be totally independent of the departmental heads.

2} Profitability in relation to Investment:

a) Margin of Return on Assets

Eg: N.P. after Tax: $750
        Total Assets: $5000

$$\text{Margin} = 0.15$$
$$i.e\ 15.0\%$$

The above result shows that every $1.00 invested in the company yielded $0.15 for the period under consideration. This rate will be compared with the rate of previous periods, as well as budgeted, to judge its acceptability or otherwise. In addition, the rate should be matched to that of the industry standard. A lesser rate could be attributed to lower services or sales volume, or lower prices, or higher direct costs and/or overheads, or a combination of these factors.

It must be noted here that target rates tend to differ from industry to industry, such as manufacturing and service industries. Even in manufacturing there will be segmentation, with varying expected return on investment rates. The same holds good for service industries, as between medical practice and providing electricity or mobile phone services. It is, therefore, important to equate apples to apples, and not apples to potatoes. In general, the services industry tend to show higher margin returns than manufacturing. This may be due to the higher investment costs needed in a manufacturing setup, than in setting up a service unit. Consider the outlay necessary in constructing, equipping and running the manufacture of Computers and TV Sets, against the setting up of a Best Buy Store where items are only procured for sale. So whilst cross-industry comparisons will be misplaced, it still makes economic sense that the higher the return-on-assets margins the better for the investor. Factoring in industry risk into returns is another issue altogether beyond the scope of this book.

b) Margin of Return on Common Stock

$$\frac{\text{N.P. after Tax, less Preference Shares Dividends}}{\text{Total Assets, less (Total Liabs. + Pref. Shares)}}$$

This ratio, when calculated, shows the yield on owners' (equity) investments only. This is much more critical and useful to the investor when related to the Margin of Return on Total Assets. It represents the portion of the income going to the shareholders. Where the rate is higher than the rate of return on total assets, it means that the owners are gaining from the use of debt capital. The reverse means that the owners are paying out more on debt capital than their contribution to the generation of income. This means that the company is over leveraged, and that management is inefficient. The essence of using debt financing is to make profits on it higher than the cost (interest/fixed dividend) on its use. Otherwise, there is no benefit in keeping that debt within the business, and management needs to get their act together, or must be held liable by the shareholders for mismanagement.

The higher the margin on investments, the better. It increases the value of the company and shareholders' worth and satisfaction. It strengthens the company against the risks of doing business, and competition. It boosts the company's stock prices and investor confidence. The rate has to be weighed against the industry standard, to assess the company in terms of its viability, profitability and competitiveness.

LIQUIDITY RATIOS:

We normally refer to physical cash as liquid, a term that everyone understands. It is the economic equivalent of the adage that *'A bird in hand is worth two in the bush.'* That is to say, money readily at hand is 'better' than money in fixed assets like machinery and buildings. Companies transact a lot of business on credit terms, and that means they create financial obligations that mature at given times. It is with cash available that such commitments can be met, and not with cash tied up in assets. But keeping cash idle in a business is not a sound financial practice, because such cash does not generate income. This presents a Catch-22 situation. This requires that a company strikes a balance between liquidity and profitability, which is done through a design for the proper management of working capital by the financial manager. So, liquidity ratios are the mechanism to assess a company's capability to pay off its liabilities as they become due. This is the test of the company's solvency, and the ability to continue in business and not go bankrupt in case of unforeseen difficulties. For this test, short-term maturing obligations are matched against short-term resources available for settling them. In essence, it is like matching a country's armies against that of a known adversary, or a football team against an opposing football team.

Of the many liquidity ratio tools, the following four will be discussed:
1) **Current Ratio**
2) **Quick (Acid-Test) Ratio**
3) **Defensive Position Ratio**
4) **Cash Ratio**

Which of these ratios will be suitable at any point in time depends on the type of company, as liquidity requirements differ from industry to industry. For instance, liquidity needs in the fast retail industry will be higher than in manufacturing where the cycle to order and pay for raw materials is longer.

1) Current Ratio

Formula: $\dfrac{\text{Current Assets}}{\text{Current Liabilities}}$ eg: $\dfrac{5000}{2500}$

$$\text{Ratio} = \mathit{2:1}$$
$$i.e\ \mathit{200\%}\ cover$$

The **Current Ratio** is often referred to as the **Working Capital Ratio.** It indicates how solvent the company is in the short term. It shows the cover the company has against creditor's claims at the time claims become due. The ratio of **2:1** above means that for every $1 of current liabilities, the company has available $2 of current assets to pay off the claim. This shows a high liquidity position that could have negative trade-off against profits. However, the method of calculation means that this ration must be viewed with some caution. The broad nature of the current assets makes some of the components not all that liquid in the short term. The current assets classification includes the following: **cash, accounts receivables, inventories, and marketable securities.** Cash is liquid by itself, current receivables are fairly liquid, followed by marketable securities and then inventories. The easy salability of inventories must be taken into account, as well as the collectability of receivables. So assuming companies A and B both have the same current asset ratio, an examination of the constituents of the current assets will show that the one holding more cash is more solvent than the other with lesser cash and more stocks/receivables.

Current liabilities usually include: **accounts payables, accruals–(eg. taxes, wages), interests payable**, and **short-term notes payable.**

A low current ratio shows a company operating in the close range of insolvency. Such a company may have problems paying its creditors, and even the wages of staff. The poor ratio may be due to past operating loses, reliance on short-term finance capital, or buying fixed assets with current funds.

The flipside is maintaining a high current ratio. This is the option that a risk-averse management will take. The trade-off is a loss in earnings and profitability.

So neither a low or high current ratio status is good, and herein lies the Catch-22 facing the financial manager, or the management of any organization, for that matter. There is the need to strike a reasonable balance. But, of course, creditors prefer a company with a high current ratio.

2) Quick Ratio

Formula: $\underline{\text{Cur. Assets, less Stock}}$ eg: $\underline{(5000-1000)}$
       Current Liabilities   2500

Ratio = *1.4:1*
i.e *140%* cover

The Quick Ratio excludes inventories that are part of the calculation of the Current Ratio. This looks at a worst case scenario that the inventories may not sell quickly, or may lose market value were the company to be liquidated. The current assets used in the formula are only the more liquid ones, being cash, marketable securities and accounts receivables. What is the rationale behind this? In terms of liquidity, cash is first on the list. Next are accounts receivables, since debtors are obliged to pay up, and the company has recourse to recover through legal action. However, ownership to inventory does not translate into receivables or cash until they are sold, which depends on the market.

The *Quick Ratio* is, therefore, considered to be a much more critical test of liquidity than the *Current Ratio*. For that reason it is alternatively called *Acid-Test Ratio,* probably on account of the quick acting nature of the chemical acid.

3) Defensive Position Ratio

A third measure of liquidity is known as the *Defensive Position Ratio*, computed as follows:

$$\frac{\text{Current Assets, less Inventories}}{\text{Average Operating Exps./Day}}$$

The 'Defensive Position' term is used because this may be likened to soldiers at a country's defence front. How long can those soldiers defend the country in times of war without needing back-up logistics and more soldiers? The funds that a company has quick access to are its cash, receivables, and securities that can quickly be turned into cash. These are the company's front defence soldiers. For the company, management may want to know how many days it can operate in the year by meeting daily needed expenses without difficulty, and without needing to seek for additional source of funding. For that reason, the *Average Operating Expenses/Day* is the whole year's expected expenses, divided by 365 days in a year. Since a company operates on day to day basis, the *Defense Position Ratio* is considered a better measure of solvency than the Current and Quick ratios. This is so because it ties assets to the expenditures required in operation, and not the total liabilities of the company. However, the *DPR* is less popular than the other two, and it is frequently ignored. It has other tags, such as *Defensive Interval Ratio, Defensive Interval Period, and Basic Defense Interval*. Could it get more confusing than this?

4) Cash Ratio

The fourth index of liquidity is the *Cash Ratio*, calculated by the formula:

$$\frac{\text{Cash, plus short-term realizable securities}}{\text{Current Liabilities}}$$

In this case, the only current assets that are taken into consideration are cash itself and short-term securities that can be readily exchanged for cash. Accounts receivables are excluded here. This makes the *Cash Ratio* a stricter guide of a company's capability to pay its debts than any of the other three ratios mentioned earlier. This ratio is suitable for a company that is on its death bed. Otherwise there is no need for a company to keep on hand cash and cash equivalents that could be invested to enhance profit-earning potential. For practical purposes, the *Cash Ratio* is redundant, and is basically of academic interest. Why so? Companies exist to make profits with other people's money invested partly in fixed assets, and pay them interests on their money. This can only be achieved through efficiency in management by operating with current liabilities in excess of the cash on-hand.

The **Liquidity of Receivables** must be factored into the calculation of the ratios, since receivables are included in the numerator as part of current assets, with the exception of the Cash Ratio. Any receivables past due cannot be regarded as current. The inclusion of delinquent receivables will lead to the overestimation of the liquidity status of the company.

Receivables are only good to the extent that they can be collected within a reasonable period of time. Where there is doubt about collectability in part or in whole, they must be included in a doubtful debt provision account.

COVERAGE or ACTIVITY RATIOS:

Picture what constitutes an activity in life. What comes to mind is doing something, and not being idle. According to *'Online Etymology Dictionary, © 2010 Douglas Harper', the word 'Active'* is derived from the Latin word *'Activus'* and means *"state of being active, briskness, liveliness."* Activity Ratio in business is a measure of how actively a company is utilizing is assets to earn profits, and with regard to liabilities the briskness with which the company discharges them. In effect, it is an indication of the efficiency in the use of the company's assets. The term *Coverage Ratio* is often used in place of *Activity Ratio* to mean the same thing. While the figures for the calculation of Liquidity Ratios can be found mainly in the Balance Sheet, the information for Activity (Coverage) Ratios can be found in both the Income Statement and the Balance Sheet. The following Activity Ratios will be discussed:

1) *Return on Assets Ratio*
2) *Return on Net Worth Ratio*
3) *Inventory Turnover Ratio*
4) *Receivables Ratios*

1) **Return on Assets Ratio**
2) **Return on Net Worth Ratio**

These two ratios can also be classified as *Profitability Ratios*, as treated above. They reveal the earning potential of assets. The more actively the assets are employed the higher will be their earning power, and vice versa. Consider two passenger bus operating companies, Maxibus and Omnibus, both using an equal fleet of buses and running the same routes and charging the same fares. If Maxibus runs ten trips a day, as against eight by Omnibus, obviously Maxibus is making more and better use of the buses (assets) at its disposal. Assuming they incur the same fixed operational expenses (excluding variable cost of fuel per trip), then Maxibus will show more profits compared to Omnibus due to more effective use of its assets. It could be that Maxibus appeals to more passengers due to offering its customers better services/satisfaction, or by having location advantage or whatever competitive edge. The sales of Omnibus will be lower in relation to its total assets, and its profits affected as a result. So lower activity, or coverage, on assets impact negatively on profits, and vice-versa. Of course, not all companies in the same or similar industries will have equal or matching resources. The industry standard ratio or rate of return, however, should be an attainable target by every company, otherwise laggards will be shunted out by the competition. So as the saying goes, every company must cut its coat according to its size, by operating within expense levels in accord with its income to stay competitive. This calls for proper feasibility studies and planning before venturing into any kind of business.

3) Inventory Turnover Ratio

The purpose of inventory in business is to dispose of them at a profit. The turnover ratio of any inventory shows its salability. It provides a clue to how soon the inventory can be turned into cash by transfer of ownership to a buyer for either cash or on credit terms. A credit sale converts the inventory into current asset as a *debtor*, which is a step closer to liquidity than the inventory itself. The ratio is obtained through the formula:

$$\frac{\underline{Cost\ of\ Goods\ Sold}}{Average\ Inventory}$$

Eg: Cost of Goods Sold   1245.00
         Average Inventory   622.50

Ratio = *2:1*
Approx. *2* times

Average Inventory is the sum of the beginning and closing inventories divided by 2. (begin + end)/2

The above computed ration shows that every $1 of inventory was turned into sales 2 times, resulting in $2 of sales. Generally, a higher ratio should have a higher impact on gross profits. But a caution: where inventory levels (the denominators) are kept low the ratio will be relatively high, but the tradeoff could be frequent stock shortages. Placing many small inventory orders could also have the same effect. In either case the end result would be worse than having a lower ratio by holding bigger stocks.

When analyzed properly, the ratio gives an indication of the efficiency of the inventory management system of the company. A low ratio could as well be due to obsolete or slow moving items still in stock. With this in mind the individual components in the total inventory have to be tested for their sales potential. Obsolete and/or slow moving items might necessitate provision for write offs. The inventory turnover ratio must therefore be taken with cautionary skepticism and investigated in more detail. When the parameters are right, the ratio at a point in time could be used as a yardstick for judging the trend with subsequent ratios – as to increases or decreases in the efficiency of inventory management.

4) Receivables Ratios

Generally, the majority of the sales of goods and services by companies are done on credit. It is only in few industries like retail merchandise, education and medical practice and others that cash-and-carry is the norm. Credit sales result in receivables, or debtors, in the books of companies. Receivables constitute current assets collectible over an agreed period of time. The liquidity of receivables depends on the extent to which they can be collected timely. There are a number of indices used in such an analysis.

4i) Receivables Turnover Ratio

The Receivables Turnover Ratio is a measure of how soon debts are turned into cash by receiving payment from debtors for goods or services sold on credit. As the name implies, it tells how many times in a given period of a year that receivables are turned over by being collected. The calculation is based on the formula:

$$\frac{\underline{Annual\ Credit\ Sales}}{Receivables\ at\ Year\ End}$$

Eg: Annual Credit Sales   144000
       Receivables   12000

Ratio = ***12 times***

The ratio of 12 times means that receivables were collected fully on 12 occasions during the year. In other words receivables were collected once every month on the average throughout the year.

4ii) Average Collection Period

The Average Collection Period shows how long it takes from the time of sales to receive the proceeds in cash. It is calculated as follows:

$$\frac{\text{Receivables} \times 365}{\text{Annual Credit Sales}}$$

Eg: $\quad \dfrac{\text{Receivables} \times 365}{\text{Annual Credit Sales}} \quad \dfrac{(12000 \times 365)}{146000}$

$$\text{ACP} = \boldsymbol{30\ Days}$$

The Receivables Turnover Period and the Average Collection Period are the inverse of each other, as per the way they are calculated. For that reason, any of them will serve the purpose. For calculation purposes where the figure for credit sales is not given separately the total sales amount is considered as credit sales. The sales of some companies may be seasonal and show significant variations throughout the year. In such a case it is the average figure of the beginning and ending receivables should be used to even out the fluctuations.

The importance of the Turnover Ratio and Collections Period is to monitor the efficiency of the management of receivables collections. They are measured against the company's credit sales policy. Assume that the company's terms of sales is 2/10 net 30. This means that payments made within the first 10 days from sale are offered a discount of 2%, otherwise the full amount is due and payable in 30 days. In such a case a collections period lower than 30 days is good, whilst a period over 30 days should send alarm signals. Steps should be taken on any such delinquent accounts to safeguard against bad debts.

The setting up of terms of credit policy must be carefully considered. A too low period means the limiting of credit to customers, which may lead them to competitors offering better terms, with a resultant loss in profits to the company. Conversely, a too generous period could lead to large accounts with some uncollectible resulting in losses. The ideal situation, therefore, is to match any such policies to the industry standard, and not to try to deviate for whatever reasons.

4iii) Aging of Accounts Receivables

Accounts Receivables should be classified by the length of time they have been outstanding. This makes for proper monitoring of the entire portfolio and focus collection efforts on long outstanding items. Here is an example of the aging % of total receivables of Company XYZ as at the year-end December 2016:

Decb	Novb	Octb	Sept	Augs	July	Jun&bf	Total
60	14	6	5	8	2	5	100 %

Assume XYZ's billing terms are 3/10 net 30 the receivables would be subject to the following analysis: 60% of receivables are current, 14% are one month overdue, 6% two months past due, 5% three months delinquent, and so forth. This is a more useful guide than the Receivables Turnover and Collections Period calculations. The Aging Schedule highlights the specific accounts that require attention. The trend over periods gives indications of the efficiency of credit monitoring, and may indicate the need for policy changes.

4iv) Aging of Accounts Payables

Just as a company is interested in finding out how quickly it collects monies owed it by customers, it also has to show eagerness in the payment of amounts owed to its suppliers. Delinquency in the payments of its debts will damage the reputation and creditworthiness of the company. However, the company can make use of monies due its creditors for as long as possible to increase the resources at its disposal for making profits. So how does a company manage this Catch-22 situation?

The standard used is similar to that for receivables, by categorizing payables by age. A schedule of Average Age of Payables is computed by the formula:

$$\frac{(Begin + End\ Payables)/2 \times 365}{Total\ Annual\ Credit\ Purchases}$$

The average of the payables multiplied by 365 days in the year, divided by the total annual credit purchases:

Eg: $\quad\dfrac{\text{Payables} \times 365}{\text{Annual Cr. Purchases}} \quad\quad \dfrac{(24100 \times 365)}{325800}$

Average Age of Payables = ***27 Days***

This data is valuable to creditors in assessing whether the company pays its debts on time. In the example calculated above of 27 days, where the industry norm is Net 30, the company pays is debts earlier than expected. This will give a favorable image of the company in the eyes of its creditors. Assuming the calculated *Average Age of Payables* is *35* days on a *Net 30* days credit terms, the company will be deemed delinquent in the payment of its debts. This will make suppliers hesitant in doing business with the company, or suppliers will inflate their prices to compensate for delays in payment. Where a discount is offered for quick payment, as on the terms of say 5/10 Net 30, the company must consider if paying on or before the 10th. day at a discount of 5% will be more beneficial compared to holding on to the cash and pay in full on the 30th. day. This can better be assessed by a review of the company's cost of capital and profit earning potential.

4v) Payables Turnover Ratio

Another measure is to compute a *Payables Turnover Ratio*. This is obtained using the following formula:

$$\frac{\text{Annual Credit Purchases}}{(\text{Begin} + \text{End Payables})/2}$$

The total of annual credit purchases is used as the numerator, with the average of the payables being the numerator.

Eg: Annual Cr. Purchases   (325800)
           Average Payables   24100

Payables Turnover Ratio = ***13.5*** times

This shows that in the course of the year the company settled its debts on the average 13.5 times, or every 27 days (365/13.5). This correlates with the average age of payables calculated earlier because the same data is used, one being the inverse of the other – one showing the length of time (days), and the other the frequency (how often).

The Payables Turnover Ratio of a company should be assessed in terms of the benchmark for the industry. A higher number shows that the company settles its debts quickly, probably due to quicker receipts of its receivables from its own customers, or cash injection from other sources making it more liquid. This could also be as a result of discount incentives offered for quicker settlement that the company considers attractive. Conversely, a lower number could indicate problems faced by the company in collecting its receivables and/or liquidity problems, or using current assets to finance fixed assets in an expansion bid. Whatever the reason, a below industry norm would not make it attractive for suppliers to extend credit to such a company. Regardless, every company must adopt the strategy that enhances the bottom line (profitability).

LEVERAGE or DEBT RATIOS:

Leverage, or Debt, Ratios examine the total financing of the company. They compare the proportions of the company's financing provided by the owners and outside sources. Where outsiders have contributed a significant portion of the financing, the company is considered to be highly leveraged, and vice-versa. So what is meant by 'leverage' in this context? Online Dictionary www.dictionary.com/browse/leverage puts it this way: *"The use of a small initial investment, credit, or borrowed funds to gain a very high return in relation to one's investment, to control a much larger investment, or to reduce one's own liability for any loss."* In simpler terms, where owners have provided a smaller amount of the capital used in the business they enjoy the benefit of profiting at the expense of the creditors (non-owners) who have loaned to the business the substantial portion of its operating capital. When the company makes high profits the creditors are only entitled to the interest on their loans and not much more. When the company makes losses and folds up creditors may lose their principal altogether as well as any claim to accrued interests. So in a high-leveraged situation the owners have the added benefit of owning and controlling the business with limited investment. Any excess that the company earns on the creditors' monies than it pays in interest is an advantage to the owners and increases the value of their shares. Picture a case where a company earns 10% on borrowed money on which it pays interest at the rate of 6%; the 4% differential accrues to the owners. This makes it attractive for business owners/shareholders to operate with as much credit as possible instead of raising more needed capital through the issuance of new shares. However, this imposes much risk on creditors. A potential creditor has to, therefore, safeguard his/her interest through due diligence before extending credit to a company. This can be done through the following ratio analyses:

1) Debt/Equity or Net Worth Ratio
2) Interest Coverage Ratio
3) Fixed Charges Coverage Ratio

Each of these Ratios is examined below.

1) DEBT/EQUITY RATIO

The Debt/Equity or Net Worth Ratio compares the amount of money invested by the company's owners to the amount of money obtained from lenders. The formula is as follows:

$$\frac{\text{Total Debt}}{\text{Equity (Net Worth)}}$$

Intangible assets are excluded from the assets in the denominator. Intangible assets are not physical in nature, and may become worthless in the event of liquidation. They appear on the Balance Sheet as assets, but their values cannot be realized to settle creditors should the company fold up, hence their exclusion. Examples of intangible assets that may be on the balance sheet are patents, copyrights, trademarks, permits, and goodwill.

Preference Shares/Stocks must (preferably) be considered for inclusion in the numerator, as debt. This is by reason that preference shareholders have prior claim on assets on liquidation ahead of **equity** shareholders. They fall in a class of lesser-secured creditors, but they are essentially creditors.

However, less conservative financial managers prefer to include Preference Shares as part of equity to better the ratio, by reason that in the worst case scenario holders of that class of shares will also walk away with nothing. Whichever way Preference Shares are treated has much significance on the ratio figure.

Below are illustrations with figures: $

Common Shares	15,000,000
Preference Shares	6,000,000
Total	21,000,000
Long-Term Debt	12,000,000
Short-Term Debt	3,500,000
Total	15,500,000

Debt/Equity Ratios:

(1) With 'Preference Shares' in the numerator -
[Total Debt + Pref. Shares]= 21,500,000
Common Shares only   15,000,000

=1.43:1.00 or 1.43x or 143%

In this example, for every $1 of owners' equity, creditors (including Preference Shareholders) are owed $1.43.

(2) With 'Preference Shares' in the denominator -
[Total Debt only]=   15,500,000
Common + Pref. Shares   21,000,000

=0.74:1 or 0.74x or 74%

In this example, for every $1 of shareholders' equity (including Preference Shares), creditors are owed $0.74.

The ideal situation for creditors would be a 1:1 ratio, where their outlay is equally matched with the investment of shareholders, or where shareholders' investments exceed that of creditors. The lower the debt ratio, the greater the chance is for creditors to recoup their monies in the event of liquidation. On the other hand, owners may benefit from higher leverage that allows them to increase their earnings without issuing new shares that will dilute their control as well as reduce dividend portions. So a company may choose to issue bonds instead of shares, with the added advantage that interests paid on bonds are tax deductible. Where a company is highly geared, speculative financial activity, if successful, will yield high benefits to the owners, while they have little to lose in the event of failure. It is believed that such a situation could encourage irresponsible behavior on the part of owners and management. A case in point is the United Bank of Switzerland (UBS) London office betting losses of £7.4 billion in 2012 that was attributed to *'rogue trading.'* The near-bust of some major banks in the US in 2014 also illustrates the situation. Those banks, including giants like Bank of America, Wells Fargo, Morgan Chase, Citigroup, and others had to be bailed to the tune of $700 billion as a result of what was described as the *'subprime mortgage crisis.'* Then Federal Reserve Chairman Ben Bernanke predicted gloomily that the sky would collapse if the banks weren't rescued. That warning led to the passing of the *'Emergency Economic Stabilization Act of 2008'.* The rest is now economic history, the merits of which will be debated for years to come.

Debt/Equity Ratio standards differ from industry to industry depending on the nature of the business and the pattern of cash flows. Banks collect monies from the public at large and lend to a few borrowers. As a result it is normal for banks to be highly leveraged. As a safeguard, they are highly regulated and monitored to maintain an amount in reserves against customers' funds held by them.

Manufacturing companies, by contrast, tend to be capital intensive and require more ownership financing before they can start operations. As a result they will tend to be low leveraged, using credit for revolving working capital needs for manufacturing inputs of raw materials, labor and energy.

Just as anyone wanting to buy shares in a company will base the decision on dividend potentials, anyone extending credit to a company should do so based on due diligence. If ownership proportion of capital is small creditors shoulder the greater amount of risk in case of the company failing. *Caveat emptor* should be the precautionary principle.

2) INTEREST COVERAGE RATIO (ICR)

The ICR is alternately referred to as Times Interest Earned Ratio (TIER). It relates the company's cash inflows to its maturing interests that have to be paid. It is a measure of the extent to which earnings can decrease and still not affect the company's ability to meet its interest obligations. Earnings before charging taxes are considered here, since interests are tax deductible. The formula used is as follows:

$$\frac{\underline{Earnings\ before\ Interests\ and\ Taxes\ (EBIT)}}{Total\ Interest\ Charges}$$

Assuming year earnings of $35,000,000 and interest charges for the year of $5,000,000; the ICR will be:

$$\frac{35,000,000}{5,000,000} = 7.0$$

This shows that the company's earnings cover its interest payments 7 times; in other words earnings will have to decline 7 times before all the company's earnings will be consumed in interest payments. This will have to be compared to the industry standard to determine the company's financial stability. Where that particular industry's standard is 10, this company will likely be rated as only fair and could face challenges raising additional funds from credit channels. The ability to meet interest payments is vital, since failure could result in legal action and possible bankruptcy.

3) FIXED CHARGES COVERAGE RATIO (FCCR)

The costs incurred by a company are classified into two categories: Fixed and Variable. *Fixed costs* are payable when they become due whether production takes place or not. They form the base necessary for production or service activities to occur. Examples are *staff salaries, rent/lease costs, insurances, advertising, depreciation on buildings and machinery, dividends on Preference Shares, and others.* These overheads remain the same in the short to long range period and are not dependent on the volume of production. On the other hand, *variable costs* relate directly to production, and are not incurred in the absence of producing units of output. Examples are *raw materials, production labor wages, production energy and utilities, and shipping costs.*

The FCCR goes a step further than the ICR. It incorporates the fixed charges into both the numerator and the denominator of the formula. It shows the magnitude of earnings compared to fixed costs. In other words, it shows the ease or difficulty for a company to pay all its bills as they mature. The higher the ratio the healthier the company is financially and contra wise. It shows how the fixed charges affect earnings, and the ability of a company to meet its interest payments.

The value of a company is directly related to its earnings. The astute long-term creditor will be interested in the extent to which his interest is covered by the earnings of the debtor company. And, in the long run, how those earnings have accumulated reserves to repay his principal. The *FCCR* is a tool to gauge a company's long-term financial soundness. It projects the company's ability to afford payments of long-term securities. The higher the number of times fixed charges are covered, the more secure it is for the creditor. At the initial stages of a company's operations, earnings may not be enough to cover total fixed charges. The company may have to depend on its own cash resources to meet such commitments. Continuing reliance on its internal cash, no matter how sizable, will soon deplete the cash stock. Thus, the cushion for meeting fixed charges is continuous earnings of enough sufficiency.

The formula for the *FCCR* calculation is as follows:

$$\frac{EBIT + Fixed\ Charges}{Fixed\ Charges + Interest}$$

An illustration, with these assumed figures: $

Earnings bf. Interest & Taxes	35,000,000
Fixed Charges	15,000,000
Interests	5,000,000

$$\frac{35,000,000 + 15,000,000}{15,000,000 + 5,000,000}$$

$$= 50,000,000/20,000,000 = \mathbf{2.5}$$

Compared to the ICR of **7.0** above, the FCCR shows a far lower figure of **2.5**. This is because the FCCR is a more cautious approach that accounts for fixed costs. With the ICR method the creditor would have that much comfort of his/her interest being covered 7 times with the borrower's earnings. With the FCCR the coverage shrinks to a mere 2.5 times. Since fixed charges are paid first, this conservative view is a relevant consideration for creditors. The clue should be a comparison of the company's actual mark to the benchmark of the industry in which it operates.

For the finance manager the caution is that increases in fixed costs not matched by increases in revenue would skewer the ratios unfavorably. For instance, hikes in staff salaries not matched by increase in output could change the fixed costs even in the short run. Changes in fixed costs must be incorporated in company budgets to match with changes in activities and production volumes.

Section 2

ORGANAZATIONAL MANAGEMENT

Examining how Good Leadership is Vital for the Health of an Organization

A Study of Organizations as Organisms within Cultures and the Implications for Leadership, with a Focus on Nestle Foods

The organization selected for study is the global company Nestlé Foods. The study is approached from the points of view of organizations as organisms and organizations as cultures. The bases are chapters 3 and 5 of *"Images of Organization"*, by Gareth Morgan.

Additionally, the paper embodies material and knowledge from my studies in other disciplines, especially *Sustainable Human Ecology* to which the organization as an organism correlates. Web material on Nestlé Foods has also been relied upon for this study.

1. 1. The Organization as Organism:

The term "organization" is widely used to refer to entities such as companies, schools, hospitals, churches, banks, charities, et cetera. The most widely known of such an entity is the "United Nations Organization", possibly because of her all-embracing and international stature. There are also the 'Organization of American States' and the

'Organization of Petroleum Exporting Countries'. It is worthwhile for good understanding to establish the basis of what is meant by the widely-used term *'organization'*. Among the definitions given by Webster's Thesaurus are the following: *"institution; association; corporation; party; body; team; group; business; society; league"*.

Gareth Morgan presents one image of the organization metaphorically as an *'organism'*. Webster's defines an 'organism' as a *"person; organic structure; animal; body; plant; physiological individual; morphological individual"*. Like any organism, therefore, Morgan posits that organizations are "born, grow, develop, decline and die."

The book, *'The Tao of Leadership'* of compiled Chinese wisdom, by John Heider, states in chapter 39 that *"Since all creation is a whole, separateness is an illusion. Like it or not, we are team players."* The organization, as an organism, does not exist in a vacuum; its success or otherwise depends on how it synchronizes with its environment and its resilience and adaptation to changing circumstances. The context within which an organization operates is the ecosystem of the organization.

1. 2. Ecosystem of the Organization

It has been established that organizations are like organisms. Any group of living and non-living things interacting with each other is considered as an ecosystem. In the case of an organization, its ecosystem consists of:

- The community in which it is located (S1)
- The physical structures (S2)
- The employees (S3)
- Governmental Agencies (S4)
- Distributors (S5)
- Suppliers (S6)
- Customers (S7)
- Other organizations (S8)
- Products and Services (S9)

Thus, according to Gareth Morgan in his book *'Images of Organization'*, chapter 3, organizations are not closed but open systems that depend *"on a wider environment for various kinds of sustenance...and* must *achieve an appropriate relation with that environment if they are to survive."* In the organizational context of modern times, much attention is given to the direct interactions with the business 'constituents' identified above (S1.....S9). Organizations invest in human resource, public relations, marketing, supply chain and other core departments within the organization. The interests of the community at large are catered to through activities in the community to create a good corporate 'citizen' image.

The organization ought to pursue policies that promote the overall ecosystem's health as each member in the ecosystem of the business ultimately shares the fate of the network as a whole.

Where the organization pursues health-promoting policies, all the stakeholders are interconnected, as per the diagram below:

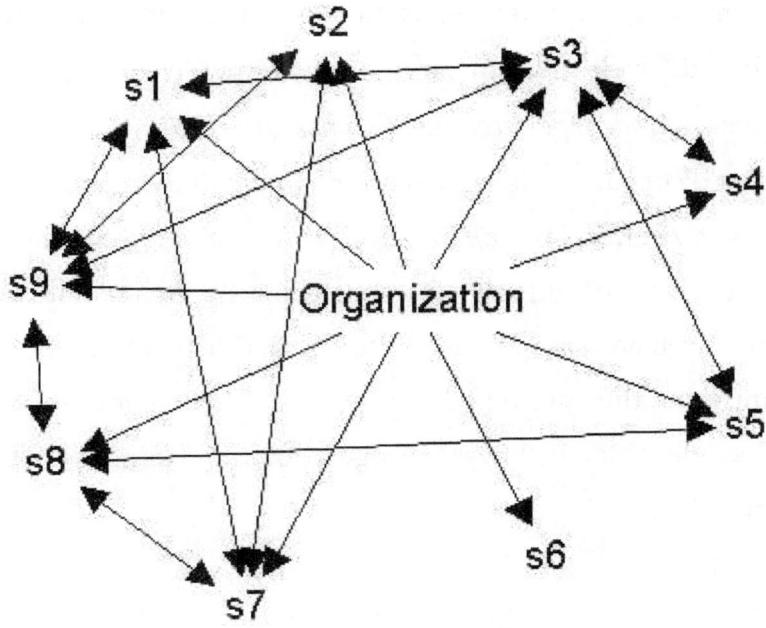

**Figure 1: Well-connected stakeholders.
(Source: Industrial Ecology)**

The result of the above is a functional organizational ecosystem where the existence of the organization is valued by the other ecosystem members. An organization well interconnected with environmental stakeholders is able to survive, grow and develop in that particular ecosystem.

One may wonder what makes an organization to blend well within its ecosystem. The website *www.goodcorporatecitizen.com states that:*

"Good corporate citizens maintain high ethical standards, decrease negative effects their company has on the environment, and give back to the community. Corporate citizenship recognizes that businesses have a responsibility to respect the individuals, the community and the environment in a way that when devising strategy they will abide by laws and regulations, and adhere to ethical standards."

Financial Management

The reverse side of the spectrum is the dysfunctional unit which exhibits a variant ecosystem diagram, as below:

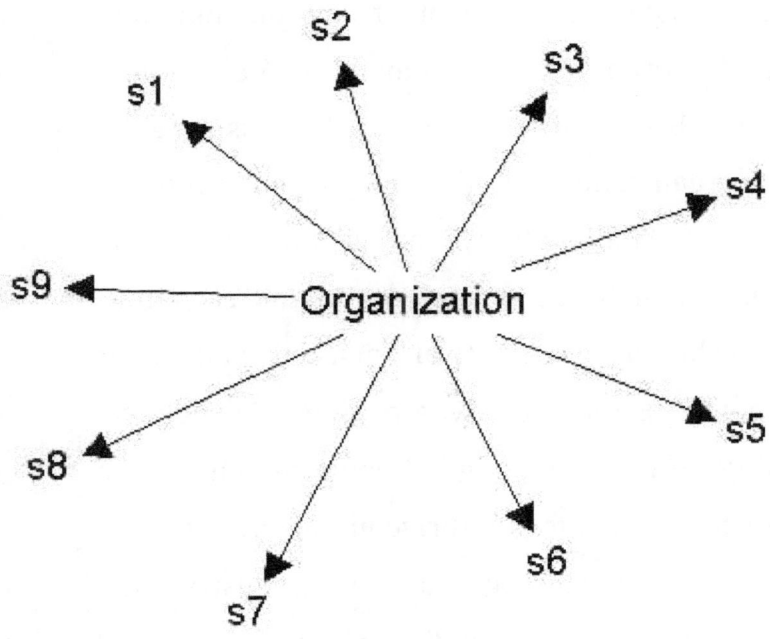

Figure 2: **Unconnected stakeholders.**

(Source: Industrial Ecology)

Such an organization is not in consonance with its ecosystem, and it is bound for quick extinction as an unconnected organism in its environment.

1. 3. Contingency Theory:

Nature is in a constant flux, and nothing remains static. The challenge to the organization is how to adapt to changing environmental trends and maintain a good fit within its environment. A *'Contingency Theory'* has been developed as a tool to ensure good fit of the organization with the changing environment. It analyses the stability or volatility of the environment in terms of changes in the economic, social, technological, political, market, and labor components. Economies where there is political instability do not foster a good environment for the business as an organism to thrive in the environment. The kind of technology in the industry, the organizational structure and employee type could create contingencies for the organization, according to Gareth Morgan.

1. 4. Natural Selection (Population Ecology) View:

There is a school of thought which downplays the organization's ability to adapt to the environment. The view is that through a *'natural selection'* method of survival of the fittest the environment eliminates the weak in favor of the fittest. This implies that competition weeds out weaker organizations, leaving the strong to dominate the market. While this is true to some extent, organizations of varying strengths exist in the same industries. Government regulations may also prohibit monopoly, thus interfering with environmental forces. Monopolies may also exist through governmental policy, as in the water, electricity and telecommunications sectors in some African countries to control prices. Thus, as Gareth Morgan concludes, *"human beings, in principle, have a large measure of influence and choice over what their world can be."*

1. 5. Nestlé Viewed in the Image of an Organism:

Nestlé Foods is the largest nutrition and foods company in the world. Yet Nestle was started as a small enterprise by Henri Nestle, a pharmacist, in 1866 in Switzerland. Henri Nestle's aim was to find a healthy, economical alternative to breastfeeding for mothers who could not breastfeed their babies. The Company's headquarters is in a small town in Switzerland called Vevey, where its striking building is sited on the picturesque banks of Lake Geneva. From that location, known as Palais Nestlé, the company has spread its influence throughout the world. Nestlé began its globalization efforts in 1905. Today it sells its products in practically every country in the world. It has set up production plants throughout the continents in every region and in many countries. As far back as 30 years ago Nestlé's globalization reach had penetrated the iron curtain with operations in far Mongolia in Communist China where the state had monopoly over economic activity. Nestlé's successful globalization has allowed it to realize tremendous growth. As the world's largest food company, it has more than 235,000 employees and 500 factories around the world. Each of the several factories operates as an organism in the community in which it is located. As an organism, each of the factories has both internal and external members. The internal members consist of the employees, the structures and the products that it manufactures. From my experience working with Nestle Ghana for eleven years, there existed policies to regulate the internal ecosystem to ensure harmony and proper operations. There were employee policies, building and machinery maintenance policies and product manufacturing policies. The external ecosystem comprised the local community and the country, governmental organizations, **distributors, suppliers, customers, and other organizations.** As an ecosystem member, Nestle Ghana had to maintain the status of a good corporate citizen. This was achieved by developing appropriate policies with regard to each of the entities mentioned above. As a good corporate citizen, the organization paid its taxes, provided customers with quality products, engaged in community benefit activities, paid money to charitable causes, and supported the national soccer teams financially for international outings. Its conditions of employment were amongst the best in the country. These activities affected bottom line profits, yet the company made good profits because of its good reputation as an ethical company. By maintaining good ecosystem balance, the organization fostered its success and the overall wellbeing of the ecosystem. The company is still thriving through good synchronization with its environment. The same is the case with other Nestle companies wherever they operate, as they all follow corporate policies from the headquarters in Switzerland. Being well connected organisms with ecosystem stakeholders wherever Nestle units operate has made Nestle Foods into the global food giant of today.

2. 1. Organizations as Cultures:

Wikipedia, the free encyclopedia, defines culture as *"the set of shared attitudes, values, goals, and practices that characterizes an institution, organization or group."* In essence, culture is the attitudes and behavior that characterize the functioning of a group or an organization. Gareth Morgan, under the culture metaphor, notes that organizations and their social context are *"intertwined in the most fundamental sense."* That means that the organization acquires attributes of the culture within which it operates. This is in consonance with the view of organizations as organisms that must be good fit with the ecosystem within which they operate. The illustration is given of organizations in Japan which are viewed as collectivities to which employees belong. This mirrors Japanese culture of the collaborative spirit of communities, in contrast with the western culture of individualism. Gareth Morgan concludes, therefore, that *"the distinctive characteristics of many other organizational societies are all crucially linked with the cultural contexts in which they have evolved."* This is portrayed by a global organization like McDonald's which adapts some menu to the host culture in which it operates, as well as providing for the taste of other cultures within the country of operation. Gareth Morgan notes that organizations are *mini-societies* that have their own distinctive pattern of culture and sub-culture, referred to as the *"corporate culture."* According to the author, the culture metaphor shows that the challenge of creating new forms of organization and management is very much a test of cultural change. *"It is a challenge of transforming the mind-sets, visions, beliefs and shared meanings that sustain existing business realities...."* Corporate culture is not static, but always changing and evolving in line with the larger environment.

2. 2. Nestle Foods as Cultures:

Nestle Foods is, perhaps, the most globalized company with operations on every continent spanning many countries. Regardless of where it operates, each Nestle unit has its authority structures and regulations and strategy that determine and regulate its operations. Variations are allowed that are consistent with the corporate culture, but not at variance with it. Thus Nestle Ghana followed the pattern and authority structures consistent with the parent Swiss company. The same organizational structures and position titles and hierarchies were conformed to in all the Nestle units I was familiar with. The same organizational code of conduct was required of every employee at whatever location, in context with the manual which was given to every employee. For each unit of Nestle, the corporate values and norms were conditions externally imposed and requiring compliance from the corporate headquarters at Vevey in Switzerland.

However, while conforming to overall corporate culture and norms, Nestle Ghana is perceived as a local company. It is seen as a Ghanaian company through the seamless blending with Ghanaian culture and the economy.

Nestlé Foods started business in Ghana in 1957 with the importation of Nestlé products such as milk and chocolates. In 1968 it began to manufacture and market locally well-known Nestlé brands. The company adapted to the Ghanaian environment by adding new products with local material content. It came out with a version of Milo called Olim (Milo reversed), later renamed Chocolim. The malt in Milo was replaced with sugar to make the product cost affordable to the average household, whilst the original Milo was also produced for those who could afford it. Corn products were formulated due to the abundance of the produce and the wide consumption in the country. Cerevita, Cerelac and Corn Meal in the form of flour are for household consumption, whilst Corn Flakes and Corn Grits are processed for the beer breweries as cheaper substitutes for malt which is imported. Though Nestle is well known for chocolate production, the company avoided the production of chocolate in Ghana due to the existence of a government-owned company which produced only chocolate. Up to date Nestle Ghana has not ventured into chocolate production in spite of its expertise in the field and the abundance of cocoa in Ghana, a prudent cultural adaptation not to compete with the local government sponsored company.

The Chief Executive Officer of Nestle, Peter Brabeck-Letmathe, summed up the company's strategy as follows: *"We want to make sure that employees at all our regional companies maintain their original cultures, but follow the same Nestle principles. We don't want to transform a Chinese into a Chilean or an American into an Australian. All we're asking for is that he or she embraces the common values that we have."*

3. Leadership Implications for Nestle Foods:

Amongst the components of the internal ecosystem of the organization is the leadership, known as the management. Management in a business organization involves the process of directing people and activities to accomplish desired objectives. The leadership function is very vital, as it determines the success or otherwise of the organization. The fact that Nestle Foods is a highly successful company speaks volumes for the leadership direction of the organization. Governance at the corporate level comprises a board of directors and a chief executive officer, and executives for functional divisions. Management at the factory unit levels consist of a managing director, a factory manager and heads of department for production, marketing, quality assurance, engineering, human resources, and general services. Each local Nestle unit as well has a board of directors exercising oversight responsibility.

3.1. Organism Image Implications for Leadership:

Nestle Foods operate in a complexity of economies and systems worldwide where it has to navigate ever changing challenges of the environment. Management has to ensure the synchronization of the company and its operations with ecosystem demands, and yet maintain core corporate image and strategies. Leadership needs to manage the challenges and complexities with high level of efficiency and business acumen. Policies and strategies with respect to each member of the ecosystem must be such that conflicts do not arise. This is often not easy to do by reason of the possibility of differences in perception of the different members of the ecosystem. A case in point was the free lunch offered by the company to employees when I worked with Nestle Ghana limited. The Internal Revenue Service considered that to be remuneration in kind, and demanded that the value be added to the workers' salaries for tax purposes. The workers, on the other hand, would not agree to the added taxation. In the end, the value of the meals was added to the workers' salaries and taxed, and then the workers were reimbursed by the amount of the tax. The same issue arose with products that were given out free to workers, where the tax component was born by the company. In the view of the Internal Revenue Service the products would have attracted tax if sold on the open market. Leadership had not considered those implications at the time the policies of offering free meals and products were instituted. The implication for leadership is that certain company policies could be challenged by other members of the ecosystem. Since the Internal Revenue Service had the backing of legislation, the company had to yield both ways as the workers were also not prepared to give up privileges enjoyed and taken for granted. The effect was leadership accepting increase in cost and reduction in profits, but it allowed for continued harmonious relations with two opposing members of the ecosystem.

Another implication for leadership is to develop the flexibility and capability to adjust to an ever changing external environment. A case in point was when the cost of production of Milo (a Nestle top beverage) went up because of an increase in the price of the input malt on the world market. Consumer complaints of high cost and reduced sales prompted leadership to come up with a substitute that consumers could afford. This was done by increasing the cocoa and sugar content as replacement for malt. The original Milo was still produced in reduced volumes for those who could afford, and also so as to maintain the known international image and quality of the product.

Indeed, due to the dynamics of both the internal and external ecosystem members, management of any organization must be watchful and alert to monitor the changes and challenges arising. As noted earlier, the company as an organism must be in consonance and interconnectedness with its ecosystem. This responsibility devolves on the leadership or management.

3. 2. Culture Image Implications for Leadership:

The cultural image requires Nestle leadership to create the kind of policies that support the cultural values of the environment within which the organization operates. This also means adhering to local rules and practices while conforming to the overall corporate culture, image and policies. The leadership policy has been to integrate Nestle units as much as possible into the cultures and traditions in which they operate. Food product recipes become closely aligned to local inputs and eating habits and preferences.

Leadership training programs aim at training company executives to develop and broaden their global mindset of other cultures. The goal has been to sensitize executives to the history, politics, culture and traditions of specific regions in which Nestle operates. Leadership must broaden its commitment to cultures in which they operate to build strong relationships with the ecosystem's stakeholders.

Being a global company Nestlé's leadership places emphasis on diversity in its workforce. Diverse individuals, who reflect many cultures, make up the spectrum of employees worldwide. The diversity policy accords respect for all individuals across all races.

The cultural image implies that leadership allows sub organizations to enjoy some-level of autonomy. Although major policy decisions are made at corporate level, operational policies are made to reflect local culture and the realities on the ground. . Nestle Foods has good leadership development programs specifically targeted at putting high potential managers in cultures that give them a high probability of success. During my tenure the staffing at Nestle Ghana was diversely rich with people of various nationalities in strategic positions working with their Ghanaian counterparts. Some local staff members went on attachment for up to a year or more at other Nestle locations or to the corporate head office in Switzerland. They also attended training courses held at the corporate office or at other Nestle offices where they met with other Nestle staff working in diverse cultures.

Conclusion:

Organizations portray multifaceted dimensions. The organization as an organism deals with the reality that an organization does not exist in a vacuum. For that reason the success of the organization depends on its relationship with the other elements of its environment. This has implications for the leadership direction of the organization. The complexity of the environment complicates the tasks and challenges of leadership in the management of the organization.

The organization as a culture portrays the organization in the context of the values, norms and beliefs and systems that affect its operations. Successful operations require co-mingling with the cultural elements of the host community in as seamless a manner as possible.

These two images in addition to the other images associated with the organization account for the complexity in the leadership of organizations. To be viable and continue in operations leadership must be able to manage the complexities posed by each of the diverse images. Leadership success is ultimately judged by the attainment of profit as an objective, notwithstanding the complexities posed by diverse organizational images.

REFERENCES:

1. Lecture Notes and Discussions.
2. Human Ecology: Basic Concepts for Sustainable Development; by Gerald G. Marten.
3. Industrial Ecology: a Path to Sustainability – L. Chalfan
4. Geography4kids.com/files/land ecosystem.html
5. White Paper on Sustainable Development and Industrial Ecology – by The Institute of Electrical and Electronic Engineers
6. Organizational Ecology – Wikipedia Encyclopedia
7. Contemporary Management - Gareth Jones & J.M. George
8. Images of Organization, 2006 - by Gareth Morgan
9. The Tao of Leadership, 1985 - by John Heider.

Re-Engineering the Dysfunctional Organization to be a Good Fit with the Organizational Ecosystem:

A Hypothetical Case Study

1. Introduction

No organization operates in a vacuum. Therefore the functioning of every organization has to be in consonance with the ecosystem within which it exits.

This paper is an examination of a hypothetical organization, 'Zonal Plastic Products Limited', from a sustainable ecological perspective. The organization will be analyzed as an ecological entity for the pursuit of specific goals. The goals are presently not met due to its dysfunctional nature of being at odds with its ecosystem.

It will be shown how the organization has been operating to date, and how a re-engineering of the organization on sound ecosystem principles to incorporate human and ethical ethos will make the organization a more sustainable entity.

The analyses will be based on these five ecological tenets:

- Change is necessary
- Diversity is needed for the health of the system
- Everything is interconnected
- Everything runs on energy
- There is no waste in nature

2. Ecosystem of the Organization

Any group of living and non-living things interacting with each other is considered as an ecosystem. The ecosystem of the organization consists of:

- The community in which it is located
- Employees
- Governmental Agencies
- Distributors
- Suppliers
- Customers
- Other organizations
- Structures housing the organization
- Products and Services

Every member of the ecosystem network ultimately shares the fate of the system as a whole. It is incumbent upon every member, therefore, to pursue policies that promote the overall ecosystem's interests. Where a non-discerning management fails to take cognizance of such mutuality, the organization is in disconnect within the ecosystem. Such is the case with Zonal Plastic Products Limited, the hypothetical subject for the present study.

3. Zonal Plastic Products Limited –

The present organization:

The company is owned by a couple, Mr. Samuel Wicker and Mrs. Edna Wicker.

The main activities of Zonal Plastic Products are the manufacture of shopping plastic bags and plastic rolls for packaging.

Mr. Samuel Wicker is the Executive Chairman, with a General Manager and five departmental heads for Production, Finance, Logistics, Engineering, and Marketing. Mrs. Edna Wicker acts as an executive to sign checks in the absence of Mr. Wicker. The hierarchical organizational structure is as below:

Financial Management

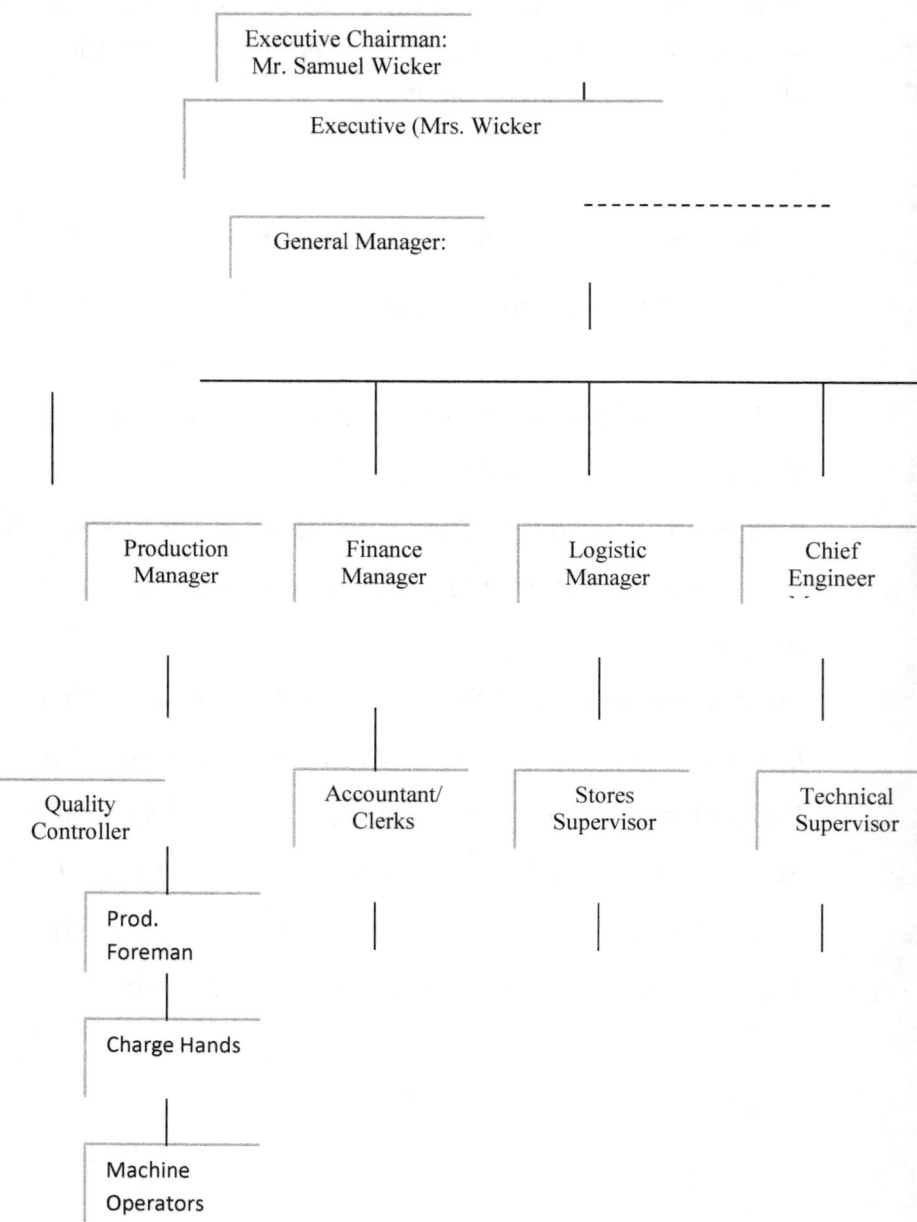

4. Diversity is vital for the health of the system:

There is no functioning board of directors besides Mr. and Mrs. Wicker.

The General Manager is a qualified and experienced administrator. The five departmental managers are relatives of Mr. and Mrs. Wicker, and they do not have the requisite qualifications and experience for the positions they occupy. Due to their relationship status, they often bypass the General Manager to report issues direct to the Executive Chairman. The Executive Chairman also does likewise by issuing instructions to the departmental managers direct, often conflicting with instructions given by the General Manager. Employees at the other levels one way or the other are related to the business owners or their friends, and lack the requisite skills. Thus the workers are predominantly from the same locality and have similar backgrounds, besides lacking the needed skills.

The result of the above is a dysfunctional internal management and operational ecosystem.

5. Everything is interconnected:

Zonal Plastic Products is not on good interconnectivity with the constituents of its ecosystem as identified in (2) above.

The reason for this anomaly is that Mr. Samuel Wicker does not recognize the earlier listed components as stakeholders. Being of little education himself, he is naïve enough to think that he and his wife are the sole owners of the company, and all the others are benefiting from their benevolence.

His views are as follows:

- The community is benefiting from his infrastructural developments and taxes.
- The employees are lucky to have jobs and not be on the streets.
- Distributors are making more profit margins on his products than himself.
- Suppliers for materials are ripping him off with high prices.
- Customers' need for the shopping bags makes him indispensable.
- Other organizations are greedy competitors, or cut-throat service providers who need his patronage to stay in business.
- Governmental agencies are tax collectors or regulators who are a bother.

Acting on his distorted perceptions, there is no human or ethical face to his dealings with those constituents. The workers are overworked but underpaid, even though many are his relatives. They are intimidated and an atmosphere of insecurity of job tenure pervades. Community consciousness and conscience is absent. There is no voluntary contribution to community welfare other than what is obligatory. There is tardiness in compliance with industrial statutes, and payments of corporate and other taxes are delinquent.

6. Everything runs on energy:

Zonal Plastic Products uses Extruders and Bag Making machines in the process of production. The machines require electrical power to operate. Human energy and skill is also required in the form of operators manning the machines. Most of the machines are old models over twenty years old and not power efficient. The lack of skills on the part of many of the operators leads to frequent interruptions resulting in more energy usage than necessary. The factory building is low in height and not spacious enough to admit in natural light, requiring electrical lightning throughout even on sunny days. In the offices the computers, money counting machines, fridges, coffee makers and other equipment require electrical power to function. The offices require lightning by means of electricity. Power to equipment is left on even when not in use, and lights are not switched off even when offices are vacated for long periods. The vehicles conveying staff and goods are old and gas consumption per mileage is high. There is therefore much wastage of energy, reflected in high energy bills.

7. There is no waste in nature:

The old nature of the machinery and frequent staff turnover, coupled with their lack of skills, lead to considerable material wastages in production. While the industrial loss standard is 0.5%, Zonal Plastic Products has been recording wastages of 2.5% and above. The losses occur in three stages: spillages of the raw materials HD and LD at the inception of production; defective plastic rolls at the end of extrusion; and defective bags at the end of cutting.

While these wastes could be recycled back into their original raw material forms, Zonal Plastic Products has not incorporated the recycling process into its production. Instead the wastes are sold off cheaply to recycling plants that recycle and resell to Zonal Plastics at a profit.

Organizational Re-Engineering

Due to the factors analyzed above, the ecosystem of Zonal Plastic Products is currently not sustainable. This fact is borne out by the organization sustaining losses in its operations for the three consecutive years 2010, 2011 and 2012. The company has operated on an ever ballooning bank overdraft for the past three years, but the bank is not ready to renew the overdraft at the end of 2013.

A re-engineering along the earlier listed ecosystem principles of *Change, Diversity, Interconnectivity, Energy and Waste* is therefore necessary and imperative to ensure sustainability.

A proposed re-engineering along these principles is given below.

8. Change is inevitable.

Ecosystems need change. Communities are always in a state of flux in order not to stagnate. There must be a change in the attitude of Mr. and Mrs. Wicker on how the company is managed. They must entrust the management of the organization into the hands of competent personnel. The General Manager must be allowed to run the company professionally and the owners exercise only supervisory role assisted by a competent board of directors.

9. Everything is interconnected:

The other stakeholders in the ecosystem of the organization must be recognized and accepted as necessary stakeholders. There must be integration into the organizational culture of all the constituents in the ecosystem. The view that they are benefiting from the organization must be juxtaposed with the reality that the organization cannot exist without them. The interdependence of all the elements must be appreciated by the owners of Zonal Plastics. The organization simply cannot operate in a vacuum. The role of the workers must especially be recognized and the conditions of service improved. This will make them loyal to the organization and lead to increased productivity.

10. Diversity is vital for health of the system:

Diversity must be introduced into the management and work force. In the present set up the departmental heads and most of the workers are relatives or friends of the owners. This has not allowed for the employment of qualified and skilled people from a diverse population pool. Diversity boosts an ecosystem's productivity and ensures sustainability. Employment into positions must be based on qualifications and skills, and the services of incompetent hired relations dispensed with.

11. Everything runs on energy:

Measures must be put in place to economize on the use of energy. The height of the production building must be raised and the space enlarged to allow in sunlight to avoid electrical lightning during daytime. Old and energy inefficient machinery must be phased out and replaced with modern energy efficient ones. The gasoline inefficient vehicles need to be replacement with modern fuel-efficient cars.

These energy saving measures require money, which the company does not have at the moment, coupled with the threat of the non-renewal of its overdraft facility. But if the company can show to the bank that it is embarking on a credible ecosystem re-engineering that will allow it to become profitable, the bank may oblige as a concerned member of the organization's ecosystem. The short-run costs associated with the new investments can be expected to yield dividends in reduced energy bills over long periods of the organization's existence.

12. There is no waste in nature:

With the proposed renewal of production machinery, the excessive wastages in raw materials will be reduced. The company must consider the addition of a waste material recycling process into its production run. This will allow it not only to recycle its own waste, but also tons of plastic waste from other sources for a fee. This will lead to considerable savings in waste materials and additional income from recycling waste for third parties.

The employment of qualified and skilled workers will also lead to reduction in wastes at all processes in production.

13. Conclusion:

Indeed, it is hard for any organization to be at variance with its ecosystem and yet survive. As T. S. Eliot puts it: *"Only the fool fixed in his folly/ May think he can turn the wheel/ On which he turns."* Organizational deviations from ecosystem norms and noncompliance are quickly met with employee disloyalty and strikes, consumer boycotts, public and press condemnation, and/or sanctions by regulatory authorities. The ecosystem, therefore, serves as a means for checks and balances on both public and private organizations. The erring organization is duly held to accountability, and must comply or die. Hence the proper realignment of the relationship of the organization with its ecosystem's members serves as the basis upon which an improvement in current practices can be undertaken. When the organizational ecosystem is healthy, it is sustainable. A healthy system is noted for its diversity, energy savings and responsible use, interconnectivity, inclination to change and the control of waste. It cannot be gainsaid that executive ethics and social responsibility and awareness are the hallmarks for any organization to synchronize with its ecosystem.

References/Bibliography

1) University Lecture and Discussion Notes.
2) 'Human Ecology – Basic Concepts for Sustainable Development" by Gerald G. Marten (1st Ed., November 2001)
3) "Industrial Ecology – a Path to Sustainability" – by Larry Chalfan (October. 1999)
4) The website: "http://www.geography4kids.com/files/land ecosystem.html"
5) "Murder in the Cathedral" – by T. S. Eliot
6) "White Paper on Sustainable Development and Industrial Ecology" – by Institute of Electrical and Electronic Engineers

An Analysis of the book

"*The Tao of Leadership*" by John Heider

Introduction:

"The Tao of Leadership" consists of passages that relate to leadership in the *Tao Te Ching*, attributed to *Lao-Tzu*, who is believed to have lived in China sometime between 570 B.C. and 490 B.C.

In his introduction, John Heider describes his book as one of China's best books of wisdom addressed to the sage and to the wise political ruler of the fifth century. In my opinion, it is the equivalent of the biblical book of *'Proverbs'* by King Solomon which offers *"instruction of wisdom, justice, and judgment, and equity"* (Proverbs. 1; 3). The Tao of Leadership is clearly an excellent basis for leadership theory and in practice. It offers many insights for leadership reflection, for strength and improvement. It draws on the order in nature as lessons for the leader to keep glued together group processes for harmonious relationships and goal accomplishment.

The introductory chapter deals with what *Tao* is and what it is not. Simply put, *Tao* means *"how things happen, how things work."* It appears to me like an instruction manual that a manufacturer provides for the practical use of a product. It goes on to state that *"Tao is the single principle underlying all creation. Tao is God"* and all living things exist because of Tao. Knowledge of Tao makes for awareness of how things happen: *"By knowing Tao, I know how things happen."* Since leadership entails broad knowledge, the leader must know Tao. This is all too familiar with the biblical quote: *"The fear of the Lord is the beginning of knowledge"* (Proverbs 1:7).

Process of Leadership:

Leadership is the process of facilitating group efforts in the achievement of objectives. *"The group members need the leader for guidance and facilitation. The leader needs people to work with, people to serve" (chapter 27).* There is, therefore, the mutual need for each to respect the other. Sadly enough, this does not often turn out to be the case as some political, business, and family leaderships and their followers operate in divisive and adversarial directions.

The art of leadership is learnt through knowing God: *"By knowing Tao, I know how things happen."* In chapter 7 the view is advanced that *"Enlightened leadership is service, not selfishness."* The leadership of Jesus in service to humanity serves as a parallel here. Chapter 2 pontificates that though the wise leader does not seek a lot of money or praise, nevertheless there is plenty of both. Such a view is in contrast with what is portrayed by those at the helm of leadership positions in politics, society, industrial and service organizations. Greed seems to be the order of the day judging by the scandals and corrupt practices exposed on a daily basis. If such leaders ever read the book they would know that *"all creation is a single whole which works according to a single principle."* The principle is that letting go of selfishness eradicates the *"illusion of being separate"* and works *"in behalf of the whole"* to the benefit of all (chapter 16). By keeping egocentricity in check the wise leader grows more and lasts longer by placing the well-being of all above self alone (chapter 7). It makes me wonder if this accounted for the longevity of Chinese leaders like Mao Tse Tung and his successors. But then we know that these same were dictators who perpetuated themselves in power through ruthlessness. By contrast, Japanese prime-ministers hardly last longer than two years, but they could be considered less egocentric and people centered, being subject to the electoral process.

The author notes that leadership encompasses some critical skills *"to assess and process what is happening within you, what is happening between you and others, and what is happening within the environment."* The wise leader allows the process to unfold on its own, but does not push to make things happen. In my view, however, the leader sometimes must provide the stimulus or push to get things done. That is why there are timelines for job completion, and the leader often requires feedback when a job is delegated. A professor may have to push his students to submit assignments within a given time. This is consistent with leadership as a process of influencing others to achieve results towards a desired goal. The push normally comes in the form of incentives, motivation, and the resort to sanctions.

The manner and quality of leadership from the author's perception is as follows: *"The highest type of leader is one of whose existence the people are barely aware. Next comes one whom they love and praise. Next comes one whom they fear. Next comes one whom they despise and defy".* This spectrum of leadership indicates the need for leaders to be humble enough to avail themselves of courses to improve theirs kills.

Nature's Principles of Force, Energy Flow, Symbiosis, Balance, and Proportion:

The book advocates for a way of cooperation with the course and trend of nature by both leaders and followers. Images of nature such as water, rivers, hills, plants, trees, ocean, and rock are amply used.

It portrays lessons and ways of life to accommodate the tendencies in nature. In chapter 1 it is postulated that: *"All creation unfolds according to Tao. All process reveals the underlying principle"* of nature. It is noted that principle and process are inseparable. It is not creation itself but the principle behind it that drives the wheel of life. Nature is in an equilibrium, since *"natural law is blind, its justice even handed"* (chapter 5). Everything is said to demonstrate the law of nature; the same principles that govern human existence equally underline all forms of life.

A good leader has the resilient nature of water. Like water, the leader is able to regain balance in no time, even during turmoil. The stream, the river and the sea are used to portray the principle of tenacity that the leader must possess. As soft water is able to wear away the hard rock, so the wise leader is able to persevere and win over recalcitrant followers: *"Gentleness melts rigid defenses"* (chapter 78). Rivers and seas are more dominant than streams, but they would not have been or continue to be powerful without the water from streams. To receive water from streams, however, rivers and seas have to lie lower than the streams. Leaders are like the rivers and the seas. They derive their power from the people, and to do so, they must be ready to stoop low. They stoop to conquer, so the title of a book goes. This is consistent with Jesus' observation in Mark 9:35 *"If anyone wants to be first, he must be the very last, and the servant of all."* Even presidents must first submit to the supremacy of the citizens by begging and cajoling for their votes before they can ascend to the presidency. They continue to be accountable to the citizens while in power, and they are removed or retained in power at the will of the people they govern. Converses in nature are used as reference points. Chapter 77 states: *"Natural events are iocyclical, always changing from one extreme toward an opposite."* Birth is juxtaposed with death; the male with female; and soft with strong. Polarities maintain balance and occur in cycles. The sun is followed by the moon, and the moon by the sun. The four seasons of summer, winter, spring and autumn complement each other in cyclical turns.

Society based on materialism and the conquest of nature works to overcome natural cycles. No wonder the disorder and chaos arising from attempts at conquest of nature, as portrayed by the ongoing oil spill in the gulf. Yet it is necessary to subdue nature for the development of society, which is a paradox.

Intuitive Strategy:

The book dwells on the metaphysical and the spiritual. Good leaders are said to be clairvoyant; they seem to know the unknown. They must *"use intuition and reflection rather than trying to figure things out"* (chapter 14). Good leaders were said to have practiced meditation. *"Meditation grounded them in the infinite. That is why they sometimes appeared deep and inscrutable, sometimes even great"* (chapter 15). The Bible relates that before the start of his ministry, Jesus went into the wilderness to fast and meditate for forty days. The leader who takes time to meditate and reflect undoubtedly is able to place things and events in their right perspective. The author advises that leaders *"pay attention to silence"* and *"learn to see emptiness"* (chapter 11).The wise leader is said to model spiritual behavior and live in harmony with spiritual values. This is the considered best way of *"knowing, higher than reason"* (chapter 72).

Conclusion:

The book promotes idealism in leadership. It is a great manual for good and fair leadership of self and others. It teaches discipline over self and ethics in leadership and conduct. It is a good resource for success in leadership and harnessing the potential of followers. There are countless insights for the leader to reflect on and employ. However, it assumes an ideal human nature, which is not the reality. The leader who is humble and yielding may be taken for a weakling. Gentleness in leadership has not proven to overcome rigid defenses. The paradox that *"what is soft is strong"* contradicts known human nature. Leaders in times of peace and in war have been known to act tough to counteract stubborn human nature. The soft and kind leader is often taken for granted. President Obama has had to flex his muscles at times to get needed legislation through congress. A tough stance by the president towards the ongoing BP oil spill crisis is yielding better results than before. This challenges the book's advice that *"the leader's job is not to direct, but to be as quiet as a guest."* Such leaders are likely to be booted out and not have second chances. President Carter is a case in point, an excellent man who was considered a weak leader. Reagan and Bush were considered tough and steely leaders but were given second chances. Solving modern man-made problems require visible and grit leadership. Nevertheless, the book is a must read for everyone in leadership, or aspiring to leadership. *The Toa of Leadership* teaches a balanced and focused leadership style for wise decision making and harmonious group interactions.

SECTION 3

LEADERSHIP IN A DICTATORSHIP

A Classic Case of Ruthlessness in Maintaining a Dictatorship

Even a Dictatorship Would Do:

Before my retirement, I usually woke up at 5:00 am by the shriek of the alarm gadget. I would still be drowsy and wished I could continue with my aborted sleep. But duty beckoned in a world crazy with the hustle and bustle of making life a worthwhile gamble. I was often tempted to call in sick, but the bills kept mushrooming in a soil fertile with needs and trifles, whilst the scanty per-hour pay rate required that I accumulated as many hours as possible. Getting to the workplace was close to two hours' travel by bus and by foot, while I was required to clock in at 7:00 am prompt. I never acclimatized to that place of drudgery where the task master of a boss reigned supreme like a dictator. It made me to wonder which was better: this humdrum life of survival or death. Up till then I often questioned the circumstance of my birth. Why was I not born to privilege with a path of succession from the womb to riches and thrones? I even imagined a dictatorship, in the North Korean style, would have been okay. I believed any god would do.

That was until the infamy of a cold-blooded murder at *Kuala Lumpur Airport in Malaysia.*

A Rude Awakening:

The callous assassination of former heir to the North Korean leadership dynasty has blown the lid off my *'privileged birth'* craving. In May 2001 *Kim Jong-nam*, travelling under the assumed name of Kim Chol, was arrested at Narita International Airport in the process of taking his four year old son to Disneyland in Tokyo. The reason for his arrest by the Japanese was probably the use of a false name. He used his real name when he left North Korea to study in Switzerland. Why then did he have to take on a false name on his excursion to Disneyland Tokyo? It was probably by reason of his birth as an heir to the North Korean dictatorship. His nobility was a liability in visiting Disneyland Tokyo. If he were recognized, the hue and cry about the North Korean autocracy breaking their draconian rules would be self-damning. And that was exactly what happened when he was uncovered. The resultant embarrassment led his father Kim Jong-il to replace him with his younger sibling Kim Jong-un as heir apparent. That led to the out-of-favor Kim Jong-nam living in wilderness homes in exile, and possibly targeted for elimination. That ill-fate, unfortunately, came to pass on February 13, 2017 in the most public of places as the Kuala Lumpur International Airport. And it was all caught on camera, staged in a classic James Bond movie style. That awful incident has given me a rude awakening: that it is not really always as rosy on the other side of the fence as I had imagined.

A Brave Martyr:

And that it might not be as bad on my side of the fence either. I, an ordinary man, can go to Disneyland Park in Anaheim, or to Disney World Resort in Orlando. But *Kim Jong-nam,* a big shot of a ruler-in-waiting,, could not be himself in going to as innocent and fun-filled place as Disneyland Tokyo. And that 'misadventure' on his part revolved a tale of woes that eventually proved to be his undoing. How sad! I looked up to him as the best agent of change in the North Korean situation of tyranny. In his book titled *"My Father, Kim Jong-il, and Me"* he stated that without reforms North Korea will collapse. That is not too hard to predict anyway, seeing that hard core communist countries like China and Russia have undertaken reforms to the extent that they are now more capitalist inclined than communist. But the late Kim Jong-nam showed remarkable courage in pointing out the obvious. It is only a matter of time. The vulture is a patient bird while it waits for a meal opportunity. So I believe are the citizens of North Korea while they wait for liberation. I mourn the brave martyr Kim Jong-nam. I hope that he rests in peace, and that his faceless murderers in high places are brought to justice, however long it takes. Were he at the helm of affairs in North Korea, the world would not have to worry about the dreaded missile threats. The kind of leader really matters, whether in a democracy, communism, monarchy, or dictatorship. The world might hail Mikhail Gorbachev because he made all the difference between him and the earlier communist USSR leaders, and the world is a better place for it. Kim Jong-nam was the best leader that North Korea never had, and the world's finest missed opportunity for peace.

Other books by the author

Muddy Waters
(https://www.createspace.com/4467610)

Synopsis

The book contains two fast-paced gripping stories. Intense descriptions immerse the reader right into the action spots and offer close peek into the lives of the characters. Valuable lessons, as well as much food for thought, will linger in the mind of the reader well beyond the pages of the book.

Muddy Waters: The foibles of society create blots like stagnant muddy waters. This satirical story raises questions about oddities that seem normal or have been taken for granted by society. The logic is to stir society's m*uddy waters;* to possibly stab the conscience of the human race at reformation and renaissance.

Twist of Fate: Official actions and policies have to be weighed on the scale of fairness and their impact on people. Insensitivity must give way to empathy. The divide between sanity and insanity is thread thin; and callousness is the sharp scalpel that easily severs it.
Through the oddities and injustices in life a diligent school head-teacher is fired for no fault of his. A benevolent former student's attempt to remedy the

situation, by a twist of fate, brings about unintended awful consequences. Will another twist of fate bring about a remedial of tragedy?

Life's Twists and Turns
(https://www.createspace.com/4294776)

Synopsis

Call it the drama of the prodigal son in reverse. Flamboyant Maulus Shane exudes chic and charm in social circles in his hometown Dorros, in the Republic of Zollara on the sunny continent of Africa. While he splurges his wealth to indulge his fantasies and pleasures he unconscionably abandons his son, Johan, to uncertain fate at the tender age of twelve.

Some years later the senile and diseased Maulus sets out to seek the now prosperous son in his time of adversity. The puzzle is how will Johan receive the prodigal father whom he least expects to ever encounter face to face?

Complicating the issue is Johan's own search for answers to the unresolved cold-blooded murder of his beloved mother years ago, for which the father possibly holds the clue. Will father and son each receive closure from the other through their mutual needs?

There is the benevolent uncle, Peter Shane, who bridges the gap between father and son in lives interweaved by twists and turns like a meandering forest path. He harbors an agonizing secret that yearns to be exorcised, but at the risk of dreadful consequences. The shocking climax catches both the protagonists and the reader unawares.

Dreams and Nightmares
(https://www.createspace.com/4476359)

Synopsis:

This book contains 101 easy to read poems aimed at making poetry an enjoyable and stimulating experience. It takes the reader on a jolly journey of poetry exploration and discovery. Poetry can be a hobby for all rather than being the preserve of academia. Those who are not used to poetry will find this book a good basis for cultivating love for it. Enjoy this extract from the book:

Erase my Errors
I wish I could travel back in time,
Turn the Time-Clock anticlockwise
Set in reverse fast motion
The seconds, minutes, and hours,
The days, weeks, months, and years;
Erasing my errors along the way
Like a school child with an eraser
Would wipe out messy pencil marks;
Perform purging surgical procedures
On my blemished past
Straightening my missteps of ages.
But alas, reversal entries,
Correcting journal vouchers
Exist only in accounting...................
....
....

About the Author:

Chrys Brobbey lives in Sacramento, California. He has a master's degree in Organizational Management and a bachelors in Administration (Accounting). He has worked with Coopers & Lybrands (now part of PriceWaterhouseCoopers), and as Cost Accountant at Nestle Ghana. He also served as Accounting Director at The Samarkand Retirement Community in Santa Barbara, California.

He is the author of two novels "*Life's Twists and Turns*" and "*Muddy Waters*", and a book of poetry title *"Dreams and Nightmares"*. His academic writings are published on the web at **http://www.oboolo.com.**

He is married to Helena. The couple has four sons: Valery, Hilary, Emery and Larry.

www.ingramcontent.com/pod-product-compliance
Lightning Source LLC
Chambersburg PA
CBHW070305230526
45470CB00002B/737